20 CIRCULAR WALKS IN NORTH & EAST YORKSHIRE

Exploring the Vale of York, the Howardian Hills, the Yorkshire Wolds and the Yorkshire Coast

Jonathan Fallis

COUNTRYSIDE BOOKS
NEWBURY BERKSHIRE

First published 2024
© 2024 Jonathan Fallis

All rights reserved. No part of this publication may be reproduced, stored in a retrieval system, or transmitted by any means, electronic, mechanical, photocopying, recording or otherwise, without the prior written permission of the copyright holder and publishers.

COUNTRYSIDE BOOKS
3 Catherine Road
Newbury, Berkshire

To view our complete range of books please visit us at
www.countrysidebooks.co.uk

ISBN 978 1 84674 430 3

All materials used in the manufacture of this book carry FSC certification.

Produced by The Letterworks Ltd., Reading
Designed and Typeset by KT Designs, St Helens
Printed by Holywell Press, Oxford

Introduction

Yorkshire is a paradise for walkers. Its three national parks (Yorkshire Dales, North York Moors and parts of the Peak District) are home to extraordinary and varied landscapes, but while these areas may get the headlines, there is so much more to explore in God's Own Country.

This book is a collection of some of the finest walks within an area of North and East Yorkshire, located east of York and south of the North York Moors. It might not be as busy or as well known as the more famous parks, but it's no less exceptional.

Get ready to discover the hidden villages, quiet lanes, sweeping countryside and coastal paths that make this a truly unique place to go walking in.

There are four distinct parts to the book:

a) **York and the Vale** – five walks, three of which are within the beautiful city of York, with a further two around historic villages within the Vale.

20 Circular Walks in North & East Yorkshire

  b) **Howardian Hills** – five walks from this Area of Outstanding Natural Beauty (AONB). Gorgeous villages and rolling hills abound here, and these walks offer tranquility and views in abundance, in a world of honey-coloured houses and great country estates.
  c) **The Yorkshire Wolds** – five walks that showcase a relatively undiscovered area of unique landscapes and solitude. This is a place of narrow valleys bisecting rolling farmland to create walks that offer variety at every turn. This is the land that inspired David Hockney.
  d) **The coast** – five walks along beautiful coastline, offering views and walking in tranquil scenery and through lesser-known seaside towns.

All the walks in the book are circular or lollipop in shape and the majority are located within easy reach of refreshments once finished. As many of the walks as possible are located near public transport routes. It is advisable to wear sturdy walking boots as some routes include occasionally muddy paths. Please note that over time the coastal landscape can change, so walks may vary but are correct at the time of writing.

I hope you enjoy these walks as much as I did.

Jonathan Fallis

Publisher's Note

We hope that you obtain considerable enjoyment from this book; great care has been taken in its preparation. Although at the time of publication all routes followed public rights of way or permitted paths, diversion orders can be made and permissions withdrawn.

We cannot, of course, be held responsible for such diversion orders or any inaccuracies in the text which result from these or any other changes to the routes, nor any damage which might result from walkers trespassing on private property. We are anxious, though, that all the details covering the walks are kept up to date, and would therefore welcome information from readers which would be relevant to future editions.

The simple sketch maps that accompany the walks in this book are based on notes made by the author whilst surveying the routes on the ground. They are designed to show you how to reach the start and to point out the main features of the overall circuit, and they contain a progression of numbers that relate to the paragraphs of the text.

However, for the benefit of a proper map, we do recommend that you purchase the relevant Ordnance Survey sheet covering your walk. Ordnance Survey maps are widely available, especially through booksellers and local newsagents.

1 York City

1¾ miles (2.8 km)

Start: York Railway Station, Station Road. **Sat Nav:** YO24 1AB.
Parking: York Railway Station Long Stay Car Park.
OS Map: Explorer 290 York. **Grid Ref:** SE596517.
Terrain: Paved roads and paths. Good for prams and dogs.

WALK HIGHLIGHTS

Wander through the streets of this historic city, passing some of its most impressive sights. York city centre displays over two thousand years of history from Roman, Viking, Norman, Medieval, Stuart and the Victorian eras. The Shambles is probably the best preserved example of a medieval street and is also thought to be the inspiration for Diagon Alley in the *Harry Potter* series. The route offers plenty of glimpses of the city's rich history but the high point has to be the magnificent York Minster, a building that dates from the 9th century.

20 Circular Walks in North & East Yorkshire

REFRESHMENTS
An abundance around the city centre with numerous cafés, restaurants and pubs.

THE WALK
❶ Start at the front of the train station, the city centre exit, NOT the National Railway Museum exit. Once outside the station turn left to follow Station Road (A1036) as it passes the war memorial and skirts the walls to then cross Lendal Bridge. Once across the bridge continue along the

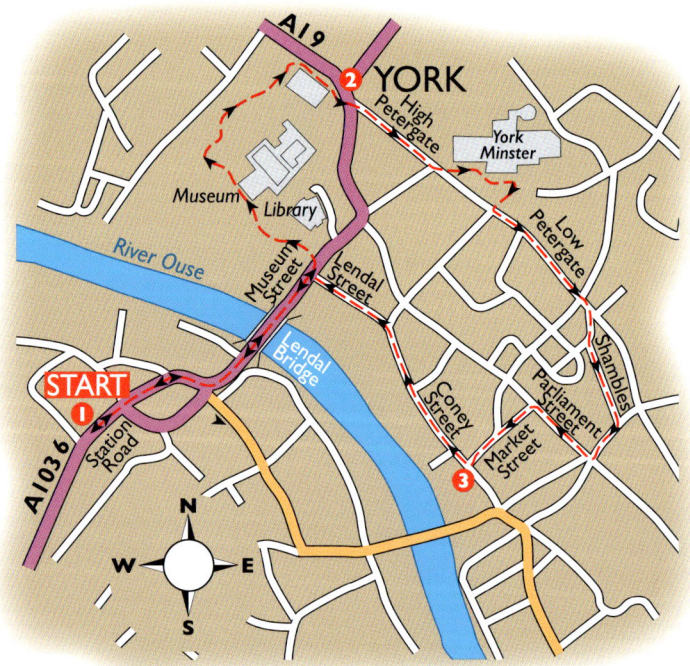

Walk 1 – **York City**

road until you reach the ornate gates of York Museum gardens. Turn left to enter the gardens and follow the path as it meanders to the front of the museum, on the way look left to see the medieval Hospitium, a two-storey listed building which is now a popular wedding venue. Follow the path as it approaches the remains of St. Mary's Abbey and then swing right to go through the arch. Continue along the path into the Edible Wood Garden, and then keep straight ahead to reach the remains of the defensive walls for the abbey. Turn right here to walk between the walls and the more modern building of York Art Gallery.

❷ Once past the gallery cross the road and go through the gate (Bootham Bar) to then walk along High Petergate to reach York Minster. Enjoy the views then head to the right of the Minster into Minster Yard. Turn right in front of the entrance down a narrow street, Minster Gates, to reach a junction with Low Petergate. Turn left, and then at King's Square head to the far right of the square to find the narrow street called the Shambles. This joins Pavement, where you turn right and then right again onto Parliament Street, the main shopping street. Once on Parliament Street take the next left onto Market Street.

❸ At the far end of Market Street turn right onto Coney Street. Keep ahead as this becomes Lendal Street. When you reach Museum Street turn left to cross the bridge and retrace your steps to the start.

2 York & the River Ouse

3 miles (5 km)

Start: York Railway Station, Station Road. **Sat Nav:** YO24 1AB.
Parking: York Railway Station Long Stay Car Park.
OS Map: Explorer 290 York. **Grid Ref:** SE596517.
Terrain: Paved roads and paths, some muddy parts if exploring Rowntree Park but good for prams and dogs. Note – can flood in winter after heavy rain.

WALK HIGHLIGHTS

Meander through this beautiful city and along the delightful River Ouse before exploring Rowntree Park on the return leg. The park was gifted to the City of York by the Rowntree family as a lasting memorial for all the cocoa workers who fought in the First World War. The 20-acres were designed to offer space for the workers of York and encourage a healthy life with amenities including a play park, tennis courts and a bowling green.

Walk 2 – **York & the River Ouse**

REFRESHMENTS
An abundance around the city centre with numerous cafés, restaurants and pubs.

THE WALK

❶ Start at the front of the train station, the city centre exit NOT the National Railway Museum exit. Once outside the station turn left to follow Station Road (A1036) as it passes the war memorial and skirts the walls to then cross Lendal Bridge. Once across the bridge turn right onto Lendal, continue ahead along Coney Street and then Spurriergate. At the junction, keep ahead and follow the road round to the right to join Clifford Street and then Tower Street. Eventually you will reach the approach to Skeldergate Bridge on your right. Keeping the bridge on your right, cross the road to the car park opposite to reach the riverside path.

❷ Turn left and continue along this path as it hugs the river. Cross a footbridge and continue for a further ½ mile until you reach a metal footbridge, Millennium Bridge. Cross this and turn right.

❸ Take time to explore Rowntree Park on the return leg. Once tired of the park continue along Terry Avenue with the river on your right. Pass

20 Circular Walks in North & East Yorkshire

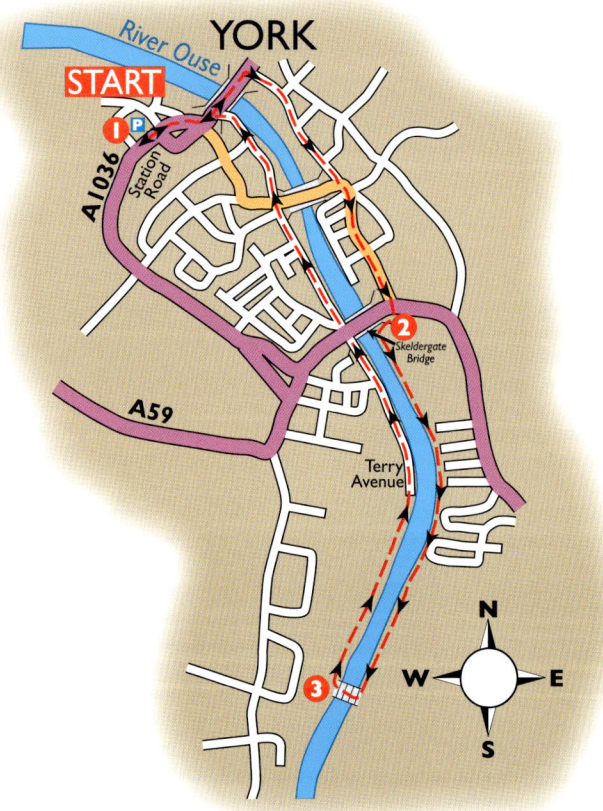

underneath Skeldergate Bridge to join Skeldergate and then North Street. In just under ½ mile you'll reach Station Road where you turn left to return to the train station.

3 York City Walls
2½ miles (4.2 km)

Start: York Railway Station, Station Road. **Sat Nav:** YO24 1AB.
Parking: York Railway Station Long Stay Car Park.
OS Map: Explorer 290 York. **Grid Ref:** SE596517.
Terrain: Paved roads and paths along the walls and through the city. Not suitable for prams or dogs. The way is well marked and there are many information boards.

WALK HIGHLIGHTS
The walk offers fantastic views of this remarkable city from the City Walls, the most complete city walls to be found in England. The Roman origins can be seen at various points but much of the route is along the slightly later medieval wall, with gaps and changes made during subsequent centuries. During the English Civil War the city was besieged by the Parliamentarians and parts of the wall were damaged. Proper preservation only started in the mid Victorian era after many parts had been demolished but there is still plenty to see today.

20 Circular Walks in North & East Yorkshire

REFRESHMENTS
An abundance around the city centre with numerous cafés, restaurants and pubs.

THE WALK
❶ Start at the front of the train station, the city centre exit NOT the National Railway Museum exit. Turn right to follow Queen Street to Micklegate Bar.

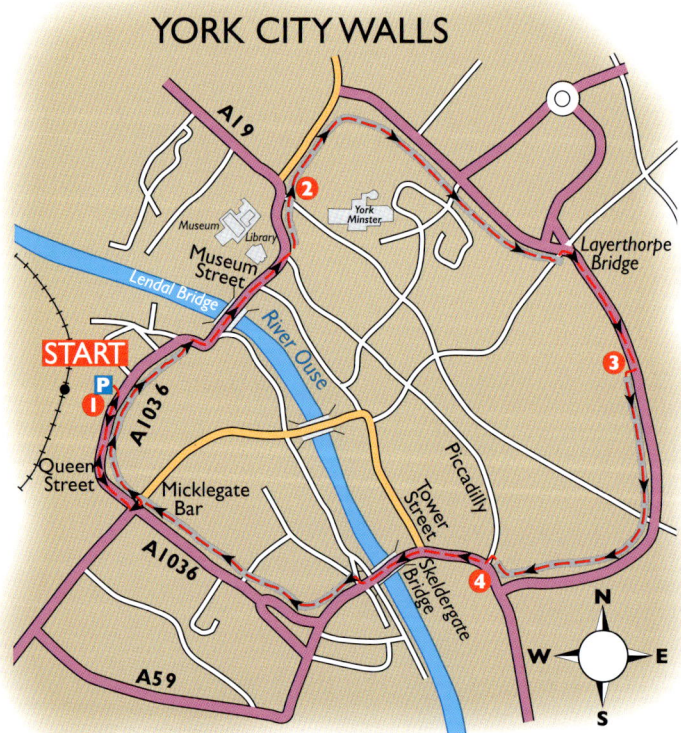

Walk 3 – **York City Walls**

Turn left, walk under the wall and up the steps on your right to access the walls. Turn right and head north back towards the station. Follow the walls to the end and descend to cross Lendal Bridge. Once across the bridge note further walls to the left, these cannot be accessed. Continue along Museum Street, following the road round to the left to join St Leonard's Place, to reach Bootham Bar to rejoin the walls.

❷ Turn left to continue north along the wall then follow it round to the right, with glimpses of York Minster to your right. At Monk Bar continue along to pass 'Jewbury', a medieval cemetery. Keep following the wall as it bends left past St. Cuthbert's House of Prayer, then ends near Layerthorpe Bridge. Cross the bridge and then head right along Foss Islands Road to reach Red Tower on your right in ¼ mile.

❸ Head under Red Tower and up the steps to rejoin the wall. Follow the walls south until you reach Walmgate Bar, the only one with an intact barbican. Cross the road and rejoin the wall on the other side. Continue to Fishergate Bar where again you cross the road to rejoin the wall on the other side. The wall bends to the right at this point towards Fishergate Postern. Next to the tower is a postern gate (defined as a concealed gate) used as a secret entrance to the city. This is the only intact postern gate remaining on the walls. The tower was used to guard the adjacent dam which could be used to flood the castle moat in times of siege.

❹ Take the steps down from the wall, turn left onto Piccadilly and follow the pavement round to the right beside the busy road to cross the River Foss. Pass Tower Street and Clifford Tower, a Norman Castle, then cross the road and head over Skeldergate Bridge and the River Ouse. Once across the river keep right to rejoin the walls on the corner of Skeldergate. Follow the walls to reach Micklegate Bar where you leave the wall. Turn left under the wall and then right to retrace your steps back along Queen Street and Station Road to return to the station.

4 Stamford Bridge
1½ miles (2.3 km)

Start: Viking Road, Stamford Bridge. **Sat Nav:** YO41 1BS.
Parking: Viking Road Parking, Stamford Bridge (free parking).
OS Map: Explorer 294 Market Weighton & Yorkshire Wolds Central.
  Grid Ref: SE712556.
Terrain: All on paved roads and paths (the main road can be busy). Suitable for prams and dogs. No stiles. Area can occasionally flood in winter.

WALK HIGHLIGHTS

It is hard to believe while walking around this small village that this was once the location of a major battle. The Battle of Stamford Bridge took place on the morning of the 25th September 1066. It was the result of

Walk 4 – **Stamford Bridge**

the struggle for succession following the death of Edward the Confessor. One claimant was Harald Hardrada, King of Norway, who landed an army after sailing up the River Ouse. King Harold, the elected King, was waiting and the Vikings were defeated. It is said that the Vikings arrived in over 300 ships but only needed 24 to return to Norway. Harold then marched south to meet the Norman-French army under William Duke of Normandy at Hastings on the 14th October and the rest is history. Although some maps show the battlefield to the south of the village most historical maps show the battle to have taken place near the current bridge. The top of the viaduct, crossed at point 2 of the walk, offers a good view of the possible battlefield.

REFRESHMENTS

The Three Cups has an attractive décor with a beamed ceiling inside and a beer garden to the front and back. The menu is full of pub favourites which won't disappoint. Dog-friendly.

☎ 01759 377381
🌐 www.vintageinn.co.uk/restaurants/yorkshire/thethreecupsstamfordbridge

THE WALK

❶ Walk back to the entrance of the car park and turn left to cross the road. Cross the River Derwent via the white metal footbridge. Continue away from the town along the road as it bends left on its way towards York. Follow the road for approx. 600m, passing the Three Cups pub, then note the raised ground off to the left, this is the old railway approach for the viaduct. Where the raised ground intersects with the road, cross the road to the opposite pavement (note cycle track signs).

❷ Double back slightly to follow the path along the side of the raised track, the path then ascends to the top of the raised ground. Follow the wide path as it then joins the viaduct over the river. Look left and the foreground is thought to be where the Battle of Stamford Bridge was fought. Follow the path as it approaches the Old Station Club where you'll find some information boards giving the history of the area.

❸ At the white level crossing gate, turn left onto Church Road heading into the centre of the village. Keep left on Church Road to join Main Street where you turn left to return to the start.

20 Circular Walks in North & East Yorkshire

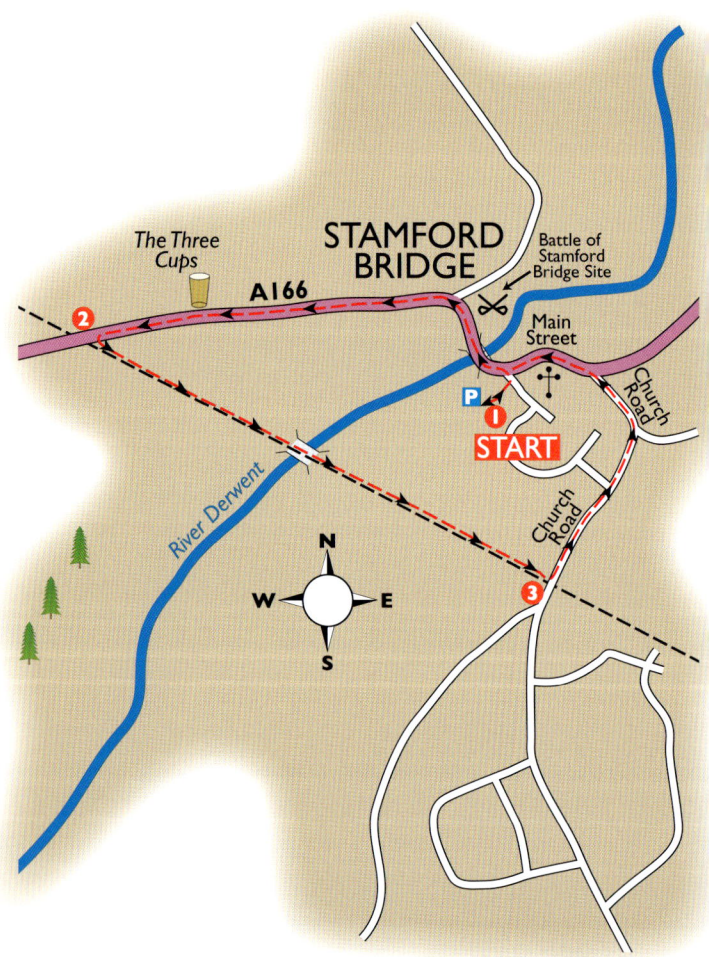

5 Sheriff Hutton
2 miles (3.3 km)

Start: The Highwayman, The Square, Sheriff Hutton.
   Sat Nav: YO60 6QZ.
Parking: Roadside on West End road or Main Street near the Post Office.
OS Map: Explorer 300 Howardian Hills & Malton. **Grid Ref:** SE650663.
Terrain: Paved roads and muddy paths, all flat. Some stiles but none would cause problems for dogs. Not suitable for prams.

WALK HIGHLIGHTS
This short walk is packed with history as it offers varying views of the castle ruins that dominate this picturesque village. In 1331 the Neville family received overlordship of Sheriff Hutton and in 1382 John Neville started to build a second castle on a new site in the village. It was completed in 1398. The first castle was a Norman motte and bailey, the remains of which can be seen near the church. It is thought that Richard III visited Sheriff Hutton several times and in 1485 he created The Council of the North which used to meet in York or Sheriff Hutton.

20 Circular Walks in North & East Yorkshire

REFRESHMENTS
The Highwayman serves locally sourced, home-cooked classics and has a good reputation with locals and visitors alike.
☎ 01347 878328 🌐 www.thehighwayman.uk.com

THE WALK
❶ With your back to the Highwayman turn right along Finkle Street. Turn left almost immediately along the narrow footpath on the left-hand side, marked with a wooden arrow (just past the sign for a bend in the road and playground). This path between houses opens up and you'll see the castle ruins in front of you. Follow the path to the left of the castle to meet a concrete drive where you turn left to join Main Street. Turn right and in approx. 300m keep right at the Y-junction, Church End, until you reach the gate into the churchyard.

❷ Go through the gate and follow a path that skirts the right-hand side of the church building. The path is clear and traces a route to the back corner of the churchyard then exits into a small wood. Walk through the wood and continue along the side of a field then through a gate into a further field. Follow the path across the middle of the field towards a dead tree where there are spectacular views all around. The path descends towards more woodland. Go through a metal gate at the field edge then immediately turn left and then right to reach a further gate and a tarmac track (Coach Road).

❸ Cross the stile and pause to enjoy the views of York Minster on the horizon, if weather allows. You are now on the main approach road to Sheriff Hutton Hall, a privately-owned stately home. Turn right, away from the Hall, to follow the tarmac drive as it meanders west with views of the castle ruins to your right.

❹ Pass Oaks Farm on your left and in 300m look for a yellow footpath sign off to the right. Turn right through a wooden gate and cross a short stretch of duckboards. This path is the Ebor/Foss and Centenary Way. Follow this route towards the village as it crosses a small footbridge and then reaches a sports field. Cross the sports fields, passing a scoreboard, then head for the large building ahead (the village hall). At the building walk towards the car park and then turn right to follow the footpath to the road (Finkle Street). Turn right to return to the pub and your car.

Walk 5 – **Sheriff Hutton**

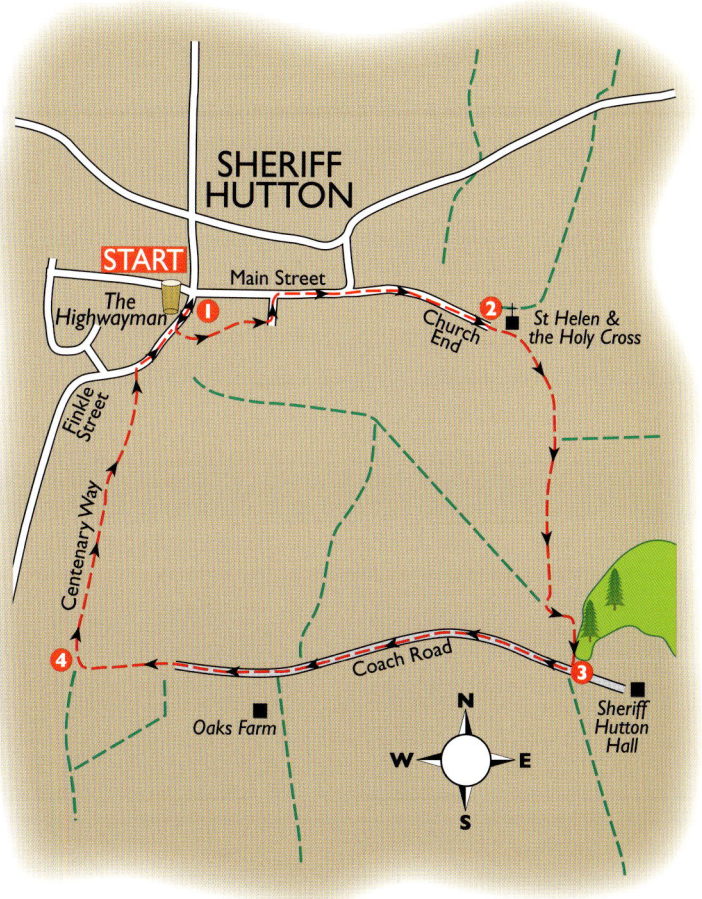

6 Ampleforth

5¾ miles (8.8 km)

Start: Station Road, Ampleforth. **Sat Nav:** YO62 4DX.
Parking: Roadside parking in the village on the main street near the White Swan or on Station Road.
OS Map: Explorer 300 Howardian Hills & Malton. **Grid Ref:** SE583787.
Terrain: Paved roads and muddy paths, some gentle slopes and fields that may have cattle. There is one stile that is difficult with dogs, they would have to be lifted over. Not suitable for prams.

WALK HIGHLIGHTS

This peaceful walk offers great views and a close look at Ampleforth College which was founded by Benedictine monks in 1802 in the grounds of Ampleforth Abbey. Its many famous alumni include English rugby player Lawrence Dallaglio, and the actors Julian Fellowes, Rupert Everett and James Norton. You'll also get a chance to see artist Antony Gormley's *Stargazing Sculpture*. This is one of many in a series of 'man standing' and is a cast of himself.

REFRESHMENTS

The White Swan offers a friendly welcome, a good menu and a roaring fire during the colder months.
☎ 01439 788239 ⊕ www.thewhiteswan-ampleforth.co.uk

Walk 6 – **Ampleforth**

THE WALK

① Walk south along Station Road, heading out of the village. As the road bends right take the narrow path on the left with the steel bars to stop

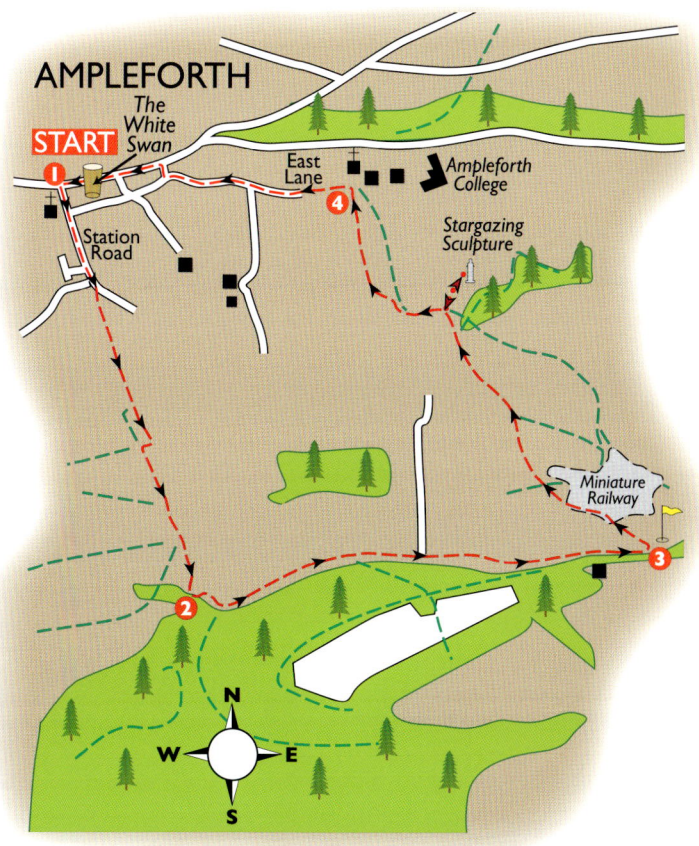

20 Circular Walks in North & East Yorkshire

cyclists. The path lies just to the right of the first two houses on the left. Follow the narrow path past a park, football pitches and then fields. Keep to the path as it bends right and then immediately left and then keep ahead ignoring the path on the right to enter woodland. Cross a footbridge and then pass through two wooden gates. Continue ahead on the same course until reaching a tarmac track.

❷ Turn left towards Gilling, following the track alongside some woodland as it bends right and then left. The track reaches a barrier and some houses, continue ahead until you reach a golf course, and then a miniature railway to the left.

❸ As you approach the miniature railway look out for a footpath sign (Ampleforth College 2 miles). Turn left to follow the path through the miniature railway then through a wooden gate into a field. Once in the field walk straight ahead to a gap in the wooden fence. In the next field keep left with the woods close to your left-hand side. At the end of the woods head diagonally right across the field to the far corner where there is a gap in the wooden fence and a footpath sign. Cross the footbridge then aim for the college buildings visible ahead. At the far end of the field you'll see a gate in the corner. Go through the gate, cross another footbridge and then a stile. Now head for the red roofed building off to the left. The path skirts to the left of some woods where you can take a short detour to see *Stargazing Sculpture*, a piece by the artist Antony Gormley. As you approach the building a kissing gate comes into view. Go through this gate, cross a bridge and then exit the woods to pass some green fencing for an artificial pitch. Follow a faint path to a signpost with a yellow sign pointing right. Turn right through a wooden gate to meet a tarmac track. Follow this as it winds to a junction with other tracks. Continue ahead and follow the track and it passes between rugby and cricket pitches. This track ascends towards the college buildings.

❹ Pass through a gate (note a footpath sign and electronic vehicle gate) and follow the tarmac track as it bends left onto East Lane. Continue to follow this track as it leaves the college grounds and passes between some houses. In a further 300m the track reaches a junction. Turn right to join a main road and then turn left to return to the start.

7 Hovingham

4¾ miles (7.4 km)

Start: Hovingham Hall, Church Street. **Sat Nav:** YO62 4LF.
Parking: Roadside parking on Church Street or pay and display parking at the village hall on Main Street.
OS Map: Explorer 300 Howardian Hills & Malton. **Grid Ref:** SE666756.
Terrain: Paved roads and muddy paths, some slopes, one stile that can be avoided, not suitable for prams. Well signposted.

WALK HIGHLIGHTS

This walk through the beautiful village of Hovingham is packed with bucolic scenery and skirts the grounds of a magnificent country house. Hovingham Hall, which you can visit by appointment, has been owned by the Worsley family since 1650. It is in the Palladian style and the walk provides views from two sides. The house was designed by Thomas Worsley and was built between 1750 and 1774. It is unusual in that the entrance is via the stable block. It is also thought to be the site of the oldest private cricket pitch in England.

20 Circular Walks in North & East Yorkshire

REFRESHMENTS
The Worsley Arms Hotel welcomes walkers and has a good menu offering soup and sandwiches along with larger dishes. Dog-friendly.
☎ 01653 628234 🌐 www.worsleyarms.co.uk

THE WALK
❶ From Hovingham Hall cross the green to Main Street and turn right. Follow Main Street, passing the Worsley Arms, as it ascends and bends to the left. At the bend, keep straight along a narrow footpath heading steeply uphill which leads to a road. Turn right at the road (Potticar Bank) and keep heading uphill for approx. 100m. Turn left at a track by a sign for Ebor Way, and follow this path uphill. The effort is rewarded with great view in all directions. In ½ mile the track descends into woodland and bends to the left. After approx. 250m you'll arrive at a slight clearing where you follow the signed footpath off at a 45 degree angle to the right. Continue through the woodland on a sunken path that descends to the edge of the wood. Go through the wooden gate into a field and follow the path through the field towards the farm.

❷ Just before reaching the farm buildings the path joins a track at a T-junction. Turn right to follow the track to a road. Turn right at the road and in approx 150m, as the road heads into trees, look left for a bridleway sign. Follow the bridleway over a stream, through a gate and across fields until it meets a road. Turn right at the road, passing Hovingham Lodge, to reach a junction. Keep straight ahead on the Hovingham path, which descends and meanders to a bridge over a stream.

❸ Immediately on the other side of the stream turn right at the footpath sign. Head into the field and follow the path keeping the stream to the right. The path crosses over a footbridge and through a gate into woodland and eventually joins a road in approx. ¾ mile. At the road turn right and after approx. 300m you'll see white gates on either side of the road. Turn left and walk over the ornate bridge to ascend to a metal gate. Go through the gate and walk to the corner of the wire fence to find another gate. Head through and follow the path right that tracks a row of oak trees. The path reaches a stile, either cross this or to avoid it turn left for 20m and then right. Follow the bridleway right towards the village. Cross the brook using the footbridge to return to Church Street.

Walk 7 – **Hovingham**

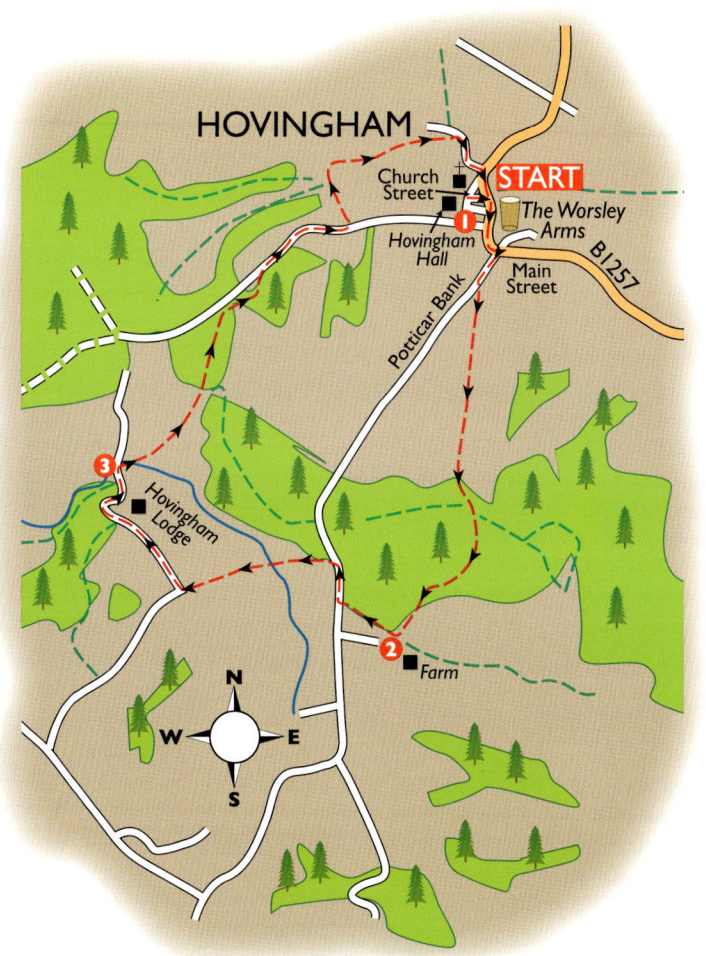

8 Castle Howard
5 miles (7.5 km)

Start: Castle Howard Estate, Mans Lane. **Sat Nav:** YO60 7DA.
Parking: Castle Howard Car Park (free).
OS Map: Explorer 300 Howardian Hills & Malton. **Grid Ref:** SE711699.
Terrain: A mixture of paved tracks and muddy paths. Not suitable for prams. Livestock may be in some of the fields depending on the time of year.

WALK HIGHLIGHTS
This walk through the grounds of the magnificent Castle Howard Estate offers views aplenty. Building of the main house started in 1699 but was not completed until 1811, the construction spanning three generations of the family. It is slightly asymmetric due to the variations in design and is very different to the original plans by Vanbrugh and Hawksmoor. Further work took place between 1870 and 1875 and a fire in 1940 forced more

Walk 8 – **Castle Howard**

restoration work to be undertaken. The house is well worth a visit if you get the chance.

REFRESHMENTS
Courtyard Café at Castle Howard (entry to the house isn't required to visit the café) where you'll find a good assortment of hot and cold food made from locally sourced ingredients, including from the estate itself.
☎ 01653 648333
🌐 www.castlehoward.co.uk/shopping-and-eating/eating/courtyard-cafe

THE WALK
❶ From the car park head away from the main house towards the Obelisk. Turn left to follow the wide grass verge as it descends then ascends towards the Gatehouse. At the Gatehouse, turn left to follow the tarmac track as it passes some houses and then reveals great views of the main house. After approx. ¾ mile the track reaches a crossroads.

❷ Turn left to follow the path and then cross a bridge. On your right you will see the family mausoleum, but you need to keep left through a field heading towards the Temple of Four Winds, originally designed as a place for refreshment and reading. When near the Temple do not follow the obvious

20 Circular Walks in North & East Yorkshire

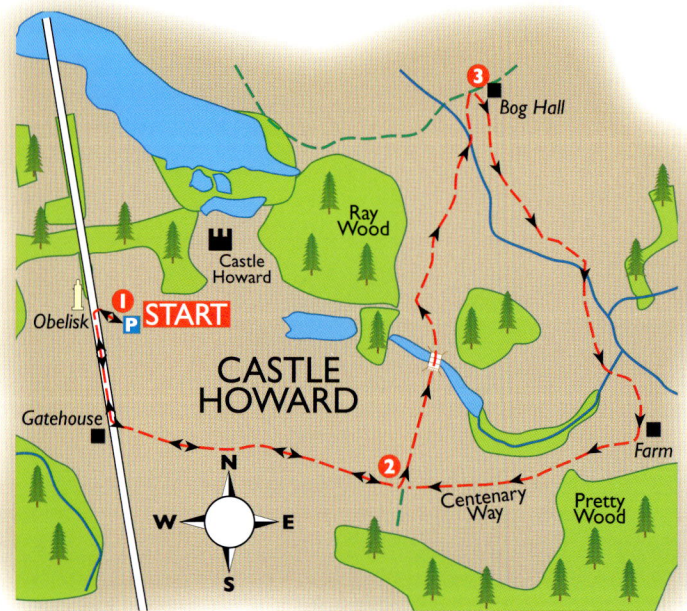

path that runs next to the wall at the top of the slope but head towards the lowest point of the field. A footpath sign will become visible, aim for this and then follow the arrow towards 'Bog Hall'. Walk towards the red roofed house in the distance. This should lead to a gate in the fence between two trees. Go through the gate and cross the bridge to reach a field. Skirt the left-hand edge of the field to reach a muddy track at a T-junction.

❸ Turn right to follow the track for approx. 1 mile as it meanders through fields, across streams and eventually reaches a farm. Turn right at the farm along a track leading to another track. Turn right again and in ½ mile you rejoin the outward path. Keep ahead until you reach the main drive where you turn right to return to the obelisk and the car park.

9 Welburn

4 miles (6.4 km)

Start: Castle Howard Estate, Mans Lane. **Sat Nav:** YO60 7DA.
Parking: Castle Howard Car Park (free).
OS Map: Explorer 300 Howardian Hills & Malton. **Grid Ref:** SE711699.
Terrain: A mixture of muddy paths and paved roads/tracks. Not suitable for prams. Well signposted with yellow footpath arrows. No stiles. Dog-friendly.

WALK HIGHLIGHTS

This peaceful walk offers great views across the magnificent Castle Howard Estate as well as of the picturesque village of Welburn. This linear village is located on the southern edge of the Howardian Hills, an AONB covering approx. 79 square miles and dominated by Jurassic limestone. This route explores some of the designed landscapes, farmland paths and rolling countryside that make the area so special.

20 Circular Walks in North & East Yorkshire

REFRESHMENTS
The award-winning Crown & Cushion, so named following a visit by Queen Victoria to nearby Castle Howard, has an excellent reputation with locals and visitors alike and we can see why. Worth booking a table to avoid disappointment. Dog-friendly.
☎ 01653 618777 🌐 www.thecrownandcushionwelburn.com
  Alternatively, try Courtyard Café at Castle Howard (entry to the house isn't required to visit the café).

THE WALK
❶ From the car park head away from the main house towards the Obelisk. Turn left to follow the wide grass verge as it descends then ascends towards the Gatehouse. At the Gatehouse, turn left to follow the tarmac track as it passes some houses and then reveals great views of the main house. After approx. ¾ mile the track reaches a crossroads.

❷ Turn right to follow the path to Welburn. The path initially gently ascends towards a wood and then descends to eventually cross a footbridge. Go through a gate to exit the wood. Continue ahead crossing the edge of a field to reach a track junction. Continue straight ahead and enter the village. The track meets a road (Chanting Hill Close) where you turn right, passing the Crown & Cushion pub, heading for the far end of the village.

❸ At the edge of the village, just past the speed sign and the last building on your right, turn right at the signed path. Follow the path as it swings round to the right and after approx. 150m turn left at the next path crossing the field. Cross a stream then go through a gate into another field. The path ascends gently towards what looks like a castle wall, skirt this and continue to follow the path to reach the outbound track. Turn left and retrace your steps back to the Obelisk and car park.

Walk 9 – **Welburn**

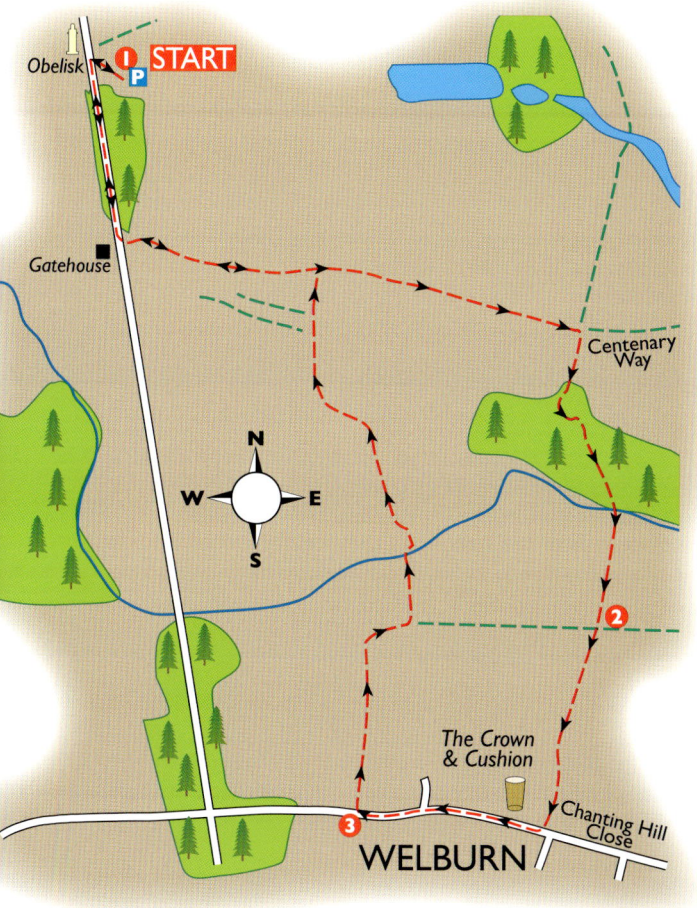

10 Old Malton

3½ miles (5.5 km)

> **Start:** St Nicholas Street, Malton or Malton Railway Station if arriving by bus or train. **Sat Nav:** YO17 9AQ.
> **Parking:** St Nicholas Street Car Park, the free car park near the station.
> **OS Map:** Explorer 300 Howardian Hills & Malton. **Grid Ref:** SE792712.
> **Terrain:** Mostly paved roads and a short stretch through a sometimes muddy park. Well signposted with yellow footpath arrows.

WALK HIGHLIGHTS

This walk around the pretty market town of Malton offers a glimpse into over two thousand years of its history. Derventio, the Roman fort passed towards the beginning of the walk, is thought to date back to the Agricola period of occupation (AD 77-83) and possibly housed the famous Ninth Legion army. This location was important for the Romans as indicated by the size of the fort (approx. 8.5 acres) and it offered great visibility across the Wolds as well as access to cross the River Derwent.

Walk 10 – **Old Malton**

REFRESHMENTS
There are plenty of options in Malton, alternatively the Royal Oak Pub & Kitchen, passed on the walk, is a popular dog-friendly pub serving locally sourced traditional pub food. There is plenty of parking opposite. Turn left out of the pub and follow directions from point 3 if you wish to start and finish at the pub.
☎ 01653 696968   ⊕ www.theroyaloakoldmalton.co.uk

THE WALK
❶ Turn right out of the car park and walk along St Nicholas Street. At Welham Road turn right towards Castlegate bridge over the River Derwent. If starting at the station, turn right along Norton Road and keep ahead until you reach Castlegate bridge. Cross the bridge and take the first right onto Sheepfoot Hill. Pass the fire station and then turn left following signs into the park. This is Orchard Fields, the site of a Roman fort and the ground still shows the excavations. Keep left through the trees to cross the park taking time to read the information boards along the way.

❷ At the road (Old Maltongate) turn right and follow it for approx. ½ mile as it passes sports fields and offers great views across the valley. Cross a roundabout and continue past St Mary's Priory church, the Royal Oak Pub & Kitchen and the Old Malton Memorial Hall.

❸ Take the next left down Westgate. Follow this lane as it passes out of Old Malton, and continues between fields. Turn left just before reaching the bridge over the A64, then follow the lane (Rainbow Lane) round to the left passing an equine hospital on your right. Head uphill to stay on Rainbow Lane. At the road turn left (still Rainbow Lane).

❹ Once past the allotments and playground you come to a junction. Cross the road to keep straight ahead along Peasey Hills Road. When the road starts to descend turn left along East Mount. Follow East Mount to a T-junction.

❺ Turn right to follow the road downhill to a crossroads where you turn left onto Castlegate. Follow the road over the river and retrace your steps along Welham Road back to St Nicholas Street or turn right along Norton Road for the station.

20 Circular Walks in North & East Yorkshire

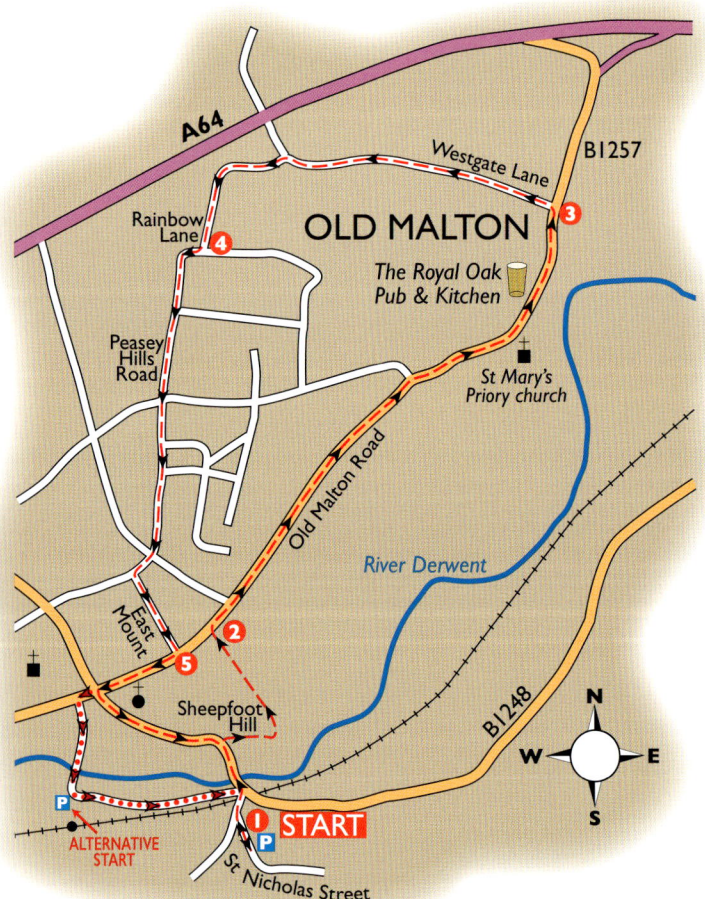

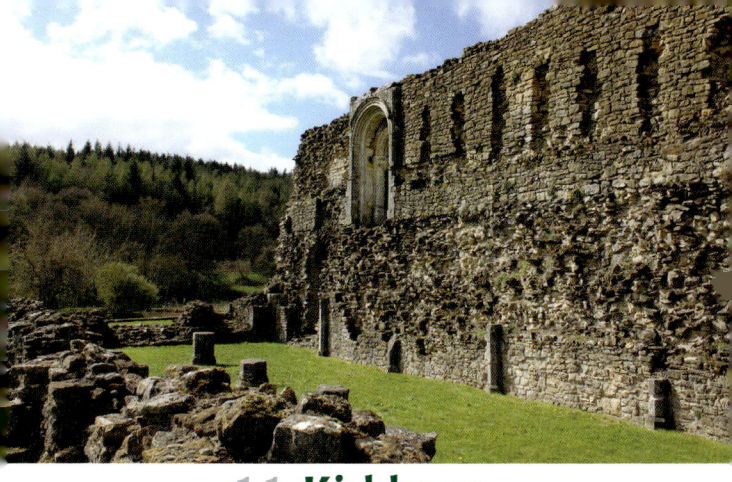

11 Kirkham

1½ miles (2.3 km)

Start: Kirkham Priory, Malton Lane. **Sat Nav:** YO60 7JS.
Parking: Kirkham Priory car park (free).
OS Map: Explorer 300 Howardian Hills & Malton. **Grid Ref:** SE736658.
Terrain: A mixture of muddy paths and paved roads. Not suitable for prams. Well signposted with yellow footpath arrows. Some steep slopes. No stiles, so good for dogs.

WALK HIGHLIGHTS

This walk offers great views across the Derwent Valley and over the old Kirkham Priory Estate. Kirkham Priory, now owned by English Heritage, was founded over 900 years ago by Augustinian monks. It was destroyed as part of the Dissolution of the Monasteries in 1539 and then was left to decay until it became a tourist attraction in the Victorian era.

REFRESHMENTS

The Stone Trough Inn is a stone-built pub with a cosy interior, restaurant conservatory and outside seating with great views over the surrounding countryside. Dog-friendly.
☎ 01653 618713 ⊕ www.thestonetroughinn.com

20 Circular Walks in North & East Yorkshire

THE WALK

1 From the car park, turn left and follow the road as it crosses the River Derwent over an ancient bridge. Continue over the railway line and turn right, immediately behind Kirkham Abbey signal box, along a footpath signed to Whitwell. This path crosses a muddy field next to a wire fence with a wood as a field boundary on the left-hand side. As the wood boundary bends left, follow the line of the trees on the faint path as it ascends through the field to a wooden gate. Pause to enjoy the views then go through the gate to another gate. In the next field, head slightly left aiming for the top right corner by two farm buildings. Go through the gate then cross the farmyard to reach a road (Shepherdfields Lane).

2 Turn left and follow the road downhill to a crossroads, there is no footpath but the road is quiet. At the crossroads keep straight ahead. The route is bounded to the left by a wood, but off to the right are great views over the surrounding countryside. When the wood ends look for a footpath sign on the left.

3 Turn left to take the narrow path into the edge of the wood and down a steep, sometimes muddy slope. This path descends to reach the road near the signal box. Turn right and retrace your steps back to the start.

Walk 11 – **Kirkham**

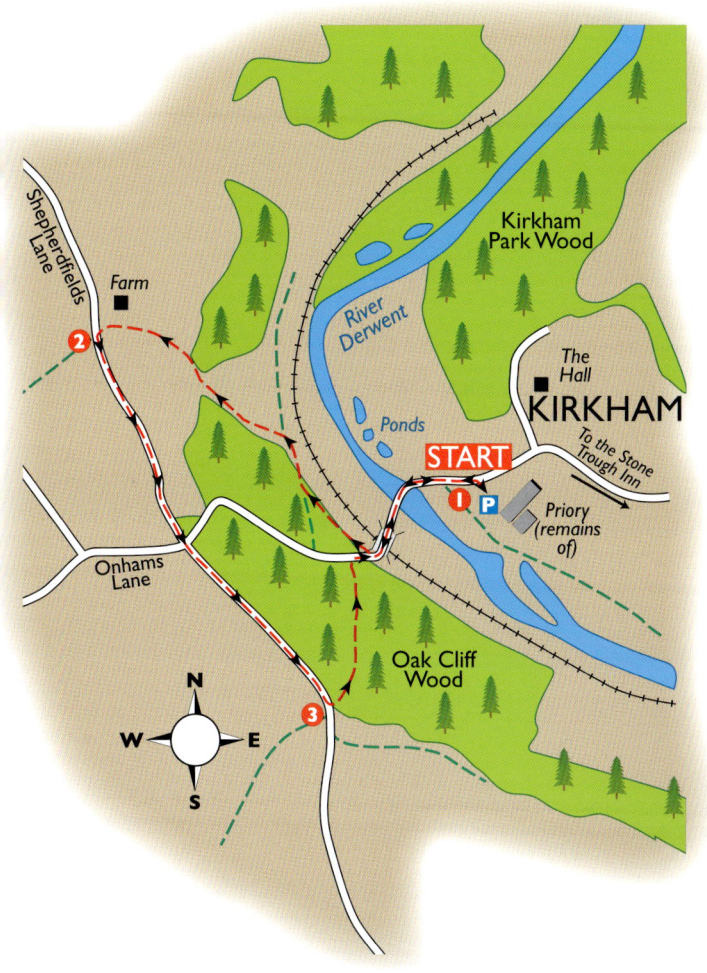

12 Millington
5 miles (8 km)

Start: Millington Wood, Wood Gate. **Sat Nav:** YO42 1TZ.
Parking: Millington Wood car park (free).
OS Map: Explorer 294 Market Weighton & Yorkshire Wolds Central.
  Grid Ref: SE838530.
Terrain: A mixture of muddy paths and paved roads. Not suitable for prams. One short stretch is along the top of a steep slope.

WALK HIGHLIGHTS
The walk offers solitude and views aplenty while meandering through this classic Wolds landscape. The Yorkshire Wolds, a National Character Area (NCA) forms an arc of unique chalk hills running from Hull in the south, to Flamborough Head in the north and stretches west along a scarp slope. The Wolds Way, a 79-mile trail, traces some of the best of this special environment and passes Millington at its most westerly point.

REFRESHMENTS
In Millington you'll find the Gait Inn, a traditional village pub with an attractive beer garden and log burner inside, serving sandwiches as well pub classics.
☎ 01759 302045 ⊕ www.thegaitinn.co.uk

Walk 12 – **Millington**

Alternatively, try the suitably named Ramblers' Rest, a licensed tea room serving cakes and made-to-order sandwiches.
☎ 01759 305220   ⊕ www.ramblersrestmillington.co.uk

THE WALK
❶ From the car park, return to the road and turn left. Follow the road for approx. 500m until you reach a point where a signed bridleway and

20 Circular Walks in North & East Yorkshire

footpath meet the road. Turn right to cross a wooden footbridge. Keep ahead on the path, go through a kissing gate and enter a steep sided valley, this is Cold Wold. The path then reaches a farm gate and sign. Follow the 'Wolds Way' and ascend the side of the valley for approx. 100m. When the path switches back on itself, follow this turn then go through a gate to follow the path as it traces a fence with a sharp drop to the left. Continue along this path for approx. ¾ mile until it descends slightly to a gate. Go through the gate and then ignore the clear path that descends the slope and follow the faint path that contours ahead to keep to the top of the steep slope. The path continues past a wood and reaches the end of the 'Wold'. Turn right to go through a metal gate.

❷ Follow the path across a field to reach a road (Cobdale Lane). Turn right and follow the road, with far-reaching views over the Wolds on your right. At the Y-junction keep right and continue ahead, passing a farm on your left, until you reach the sign for Warren Farm. Turn right and follow the drive to a hedge of trees where the track turns sharply left.

❸ Turn right here and head along the Wolds Way as it follows the top edge of the field and then turns left to gently descend to a gate. Go through the gate and then continue to descend into Cold Wold. The path descends to rejoin the outbound route where you turn left and retrace your steps back to the road. Turn left at the road to return to the start.

13 Huggate
5 miles (8 km)

Start: Huggate Car Park, Driffield Road. **Sat Nav:** YO42 1YH.
Parking: Huggate Car Park (free) which lies just to the east of the Wolds Inn pub.
OS Map: Explorer 294 Market Weighton & Yorkshire Wolds Central.
  Grid Ref: SE884550.
Terrain: Paved roads and muddy paths, some slopes, no stiles but cattle can be in some of the fields at some points of the year. Not suitable for prams.

WALK HIGHLIGHTS
This walk starts at the highest village in the Wolds and passes through some of the finest countryside the area has to offer with far-reaching views across three valleys.

Huggate Poetry Bench, passed on the walk, is one of six sculpted benches created as part of the WANDER art project, a project set up to install a variety of artwork along the Yorkshire Wolds Way. The bench was designed by artist Angus Ross and is carved with a poem by John Clark.

20 Circular Walks in North & East Yorkshire

REFRESHMENTS
Wolds Inn, said to be the highest pub in the Wolds, welcomes walkers with a hearty menu served in the bar, restaurant or beer garden. Dog-friendly.
☎ 01377 288217 ⊕ www.woldsinn.com

THE WALK

❶ Turn right out of the car park, passing Wolds Inn to reach a crossroads. Turn right along Stocks Hill which soon becomes Church Street and follow signs into the village proper. Follow the road as it descends and eventually leaves the houses behind to become a sunken lane. Keep ahead past the sign for Glebe Farm on your left and soon the lane starts to ascend while the fields and views open out. Continue along the lane to the highest point where there is a track junction before a farm.

❷ Turn left following the sign for the Wolds Way and head along the edge of the field. The track then reaches a gate. Go through the gate and turn right to descend to an ornate bench, Huggate Poetry Bench. This is Horse Dale. The ridge on which the gate is located is thought to be part of widespread Bronze Age earthworks, which have baffled scientists in terms of their size and location. From the bench you'll see one of the finest views of the unique Wolds landscape along with Horse, Holm and Harper Dale. Follow the path as it gently descends to the bottom of Horse Dale to reach a set of metal gates. Ignore the Wolds Way sign and instead go through the gate to the right, there is no sign but there is evidence of a trodden route. Follow the path along the meandering dale as it ascends to a cattle grid/farm gate located at end of a wood on the right-hand side. Go over the cattle grid and follow the farm track to a sharp right-hand bend. Just past the bend you'll see a footpath sign off to the left.

❸ Turn left to follow the footpath as it descends into another dale, Rabbit Dale. At the bottom, turn right to follow the path through a metal gate. Continue along the meandering valley until you reach a wooden farm gate. At this gate take the signed footpath to the right and follow a side valley that leads to a further farm gate that returns to the outbound lane. Turn left and retrace your steps through the village and then left again at the crossroads to return to the car park.

Walk 13 – **Huggate**

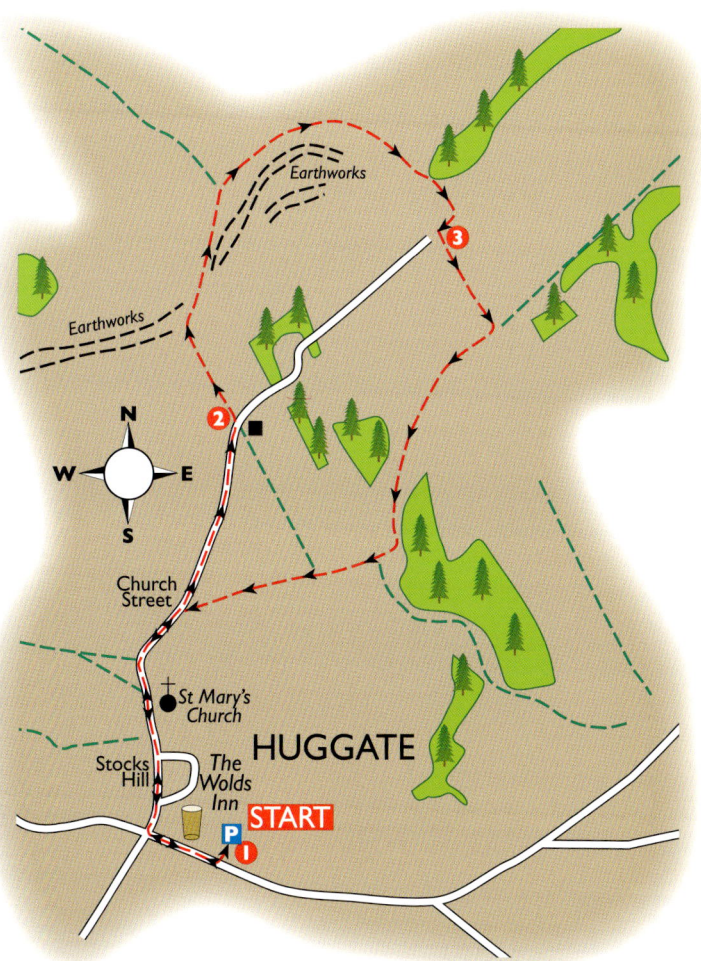

14 Wharram Percy

2¾ miles (4.4 km)

Start: Wharram Percy English Heritage Car Park. **Sat Nav:** YO17 9TD.
Parking: Wharram Percy English Heritage Car Park.
OS Map: Explorer 300 Howardian Hills & Malton. **Grid Ref:** SE867644.
Terrain: Paved roads and muddy paths, some steep-sided slopes. No stiles but cattle may be in some of the fields. Not suitable for prams.

WALK HIGHLIGHTS

The walk takes you through the ancient settlement of Wharram Percy, one of the best preserved deserted medieval villages in the UK. Managed by English Heritage, extensive research over the years has proved vital to our understanding of what day-to-day life might have been like for medieval communities. The village was eventually abandoned in the 16th century. It is thought likely that the occupants were evicted to make way for sheep farming, an early example of clearances as part of the agricultural revolution.

Walk 14 – **Wharram Percy**

REFRESHMENTS
None on the walk. The nearest pubs are either the Cross Keys in Thixendale or The Jolly Farmer Inn in Leavening, both around 6 miles away.

THE WALK

❶ Head out of the car park and turn right along the road with spectacular views in all directions. Follow this straight road slightly uphill for around ¾ mile. Eventually the road does a dog leg and at this point you turn right through a gateway to leave the road and join the signed Centenary Way. Follow the track as it passes woodland on the right and continues along the edge of fields next to a hedge. This track then starts to gently descend and reaches a metal farm gate.

❷ Go through the gate and turn right to follow the path along the top of a steep-sided valley, this is Deep Dale. After approx. ¾ mile the path descends towards what was once a medieval village. All that remains is the millpond, the outline of a number of houses and the ruins of the church. Go through the gate and past the millpond, keeping it to your left. Follow the path past the church and then keep to the left of the boarded up building, once used as an archaeological research base. The path then descends into

20 Circular Walks in North & East Yorkshire

woodland. At the river turn right to cross the bridge and go through a gate into a field. Cross the field, go through a further gate and then follow a sunken path as it ascends back to the start point.

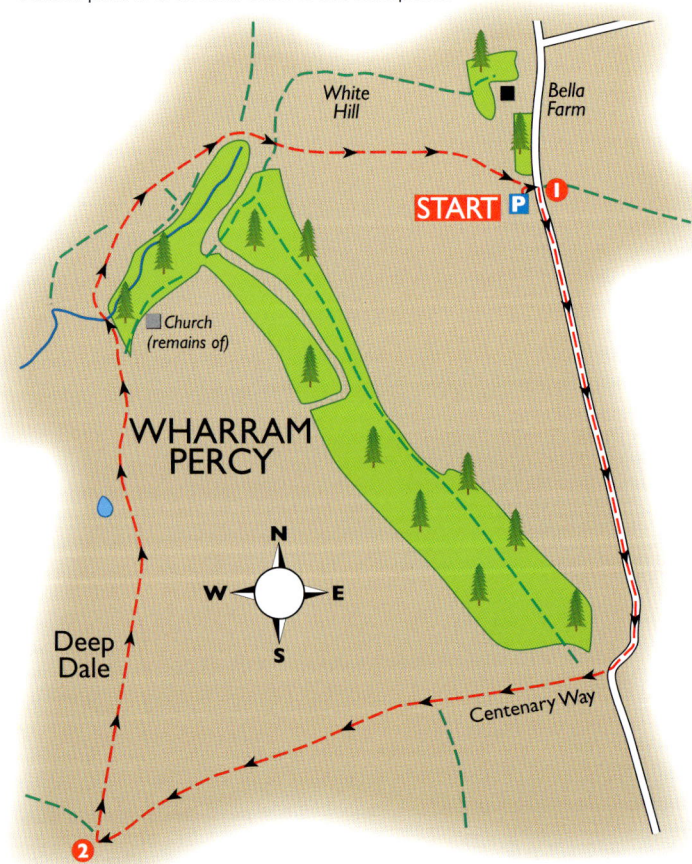

15 Driffield & the Croom Mabel Trod

3 miles (4.7 km)

Start: Mill Street, Driffield. **Sat Nav:** YO25 6RQ.
Parking: Cross Hill Car Park on Mill Street.
OS Map: Explorer 294 Market Weighton & Yorkshire Wolds Central.
  Grid Ref: TA023576.
Terrain: A mixture of paved tracks and pavements with a short part through a muddy park. Suitable for dogs and prams.

WALK HIGHLIGHTS

The walk starts in the market town of Driffield, known as the Capital of the Wolds due to its location in the centre of it. The route soon heads to the outskirts of the town and traces the footsteps of one of the Wold Rangers. Croom Mabel was born in Little Driffield, and from childhood made a living roaming the lanes around the town collecting old clothes from the local farmers, piling them into a pram (which earned her the nickname 'Queen of the Pram Pushers') and selling them at the rag merchant. She was one

20 Circular Walks in North & East Yorkshire

of many women and men who became known as the Wold Rangers, a group of nomadic agricultural labourers whose work dried up following the introduction of machinery on farms. The walk traces one of her well-known routes.

REFRESHMENTS
Head to Market Place for a good choice of cafés and restaurants.

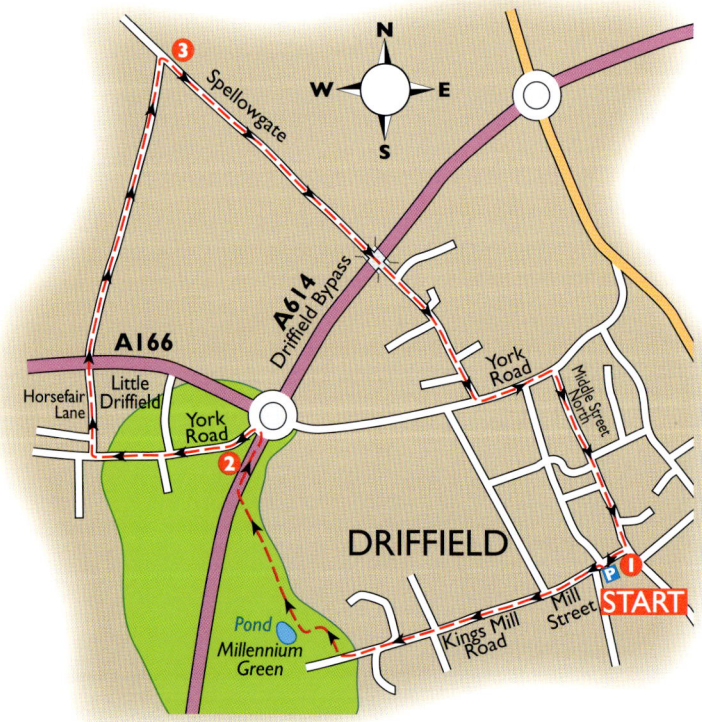

Walk 15 – Driffield & the Croom Mabel Trod

THE WALK

1 Turn left out of the car park and head down Mill Street, keep ahead as the road swings right to join Kings Mill Road. You soon pass the cricket club on the left. When the road swings to the left keep ahead to stay on Kings Mill Road to reach a green space to your right, Millennium Green. Go through the gate and follow the path as it curves left to pass the pond. At the pond turn right to follow another path that goes north toward a 20m-high tree stump. Pass the stump and follow the path through woodland to reach the road (A614/ Driffield Bypass). Turn right towards the roundabout.

2 Cross over at the crossing and keep straight through a railing gap to York Road heading towards Little Driffield. Continue through the village until you reach Horsefair Lane off to the right. In 200m you will reach the A166 which you cross with care to follow a track opposite signed unsuitable for motors. The track gently ascends and passes a dog exercise field. Join another single track road at a T-junction, this is Spellowgate.

3 Join another single track road (Spellowgate) at a T-junction where you turn right. Follow this road back into Driffield, passing the Great Driffield sign and crossing a bridge over the A614. Keep ahead along Spellowgate past houses to reach a T-junction. Turn left onto York Road which soon becomes North Street. Then take the second turning on the right onto Middle Street North. At the roundabout turn right onto Mill Street to return to the start.

16 Filey Brigg

3 miles (5 km)

Start: Filey Railway Station or Station Avenue Car Park.
  Sat Nav: YO14 9PE.
Parking: Station Avenue Car Park (pay & display) or park along the seafront (The Beach, YO14 9LA) and start from point 3 of the walk.
OS Map: Explorer 301 Scarborough, Bridlington & Flamborough Head.
  Grid Ref: TA115807.
Terrain: A mixture of muddy tracks and paved roads. Not suitable for prams. Well signposted. Good for dogs.

WALK HIGHLIGHTS

This is a wonderful walk around the seaside town of Filey, offering great views along the Yorkshire coast and a chance to explore the Country Park as well as Filey Brigg, a long narrow peninsular which has been designated a Site of Special Scientific Interest.

Walk 16 – **Filey Brigg**

REFRESHMENTS
Lots of options in the town but we would recommend The Glass House at Charlotte's passed on the walk on Belle Vue Street. Here you'll find a good menu along with plenty of seafood specials.
☎ 01723 447400 ⊕ www.theglasshouseatcharlottes.co.uk

THE WALK
❶ From the station, head along Station Approach to reach a roundabout. From the car park just make your way back to the main road and you'll see the roundabout ahead. Cross the road with care to join Station Road on the opposite side. Keep ahead to another roundabout where you turn right and then immediately left along Church Street. As the road bends round to the right keep straight ahead by the dead-end road sign to stay on Church Street. Cross the bridge at the end to approach Saint Oswald's Church. Keep left and

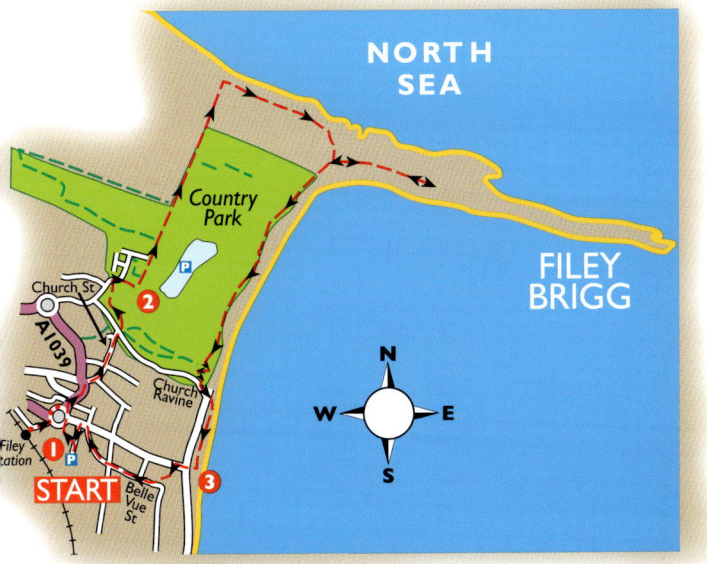

20 Circular Walks in North & East Yorkshire

follow the path to meet a lane where you turn left following the sign for the Country Park. Just before you reach the main road (Church Cliff Drive) turn right along the path to cross the green. Follow the road as it bends round to the right and head past Brigg Court on your left. Look out for a path on your left opposite gated Church Cliff Farm. Don't take the path that runs immediately alongside Brigg Court but take the next one, which runs parallel and is initially through trees near a blue bin.

❷ This path runs alongside the Country Park, and eventually reaches the cliffs at a T-junction. Turn right along this coastal clifftop path, the Cleveland Way. In 300m you'll reach the Stone Marker, marking the entrance to Filey Brigg. Turn left to explore this narrow peninsular and then return to the marker and turn left to continue the walk. Keep ahead through the Country Park, sticking to the coastal path, then zigzagging through the trees on steps to reach a track with Filey Sailing Club to your left. Keep ahead on the coastal path to the far end of the park where the path again enters a wood. Zigzag down more concrete steps to reach Church Ravine by some public toilets. Turn left to join the seafront promenade.

❸ Follow the promenade to the public toilets and a café, where you will see some steps up to the main road. Cross the road and walk up Cargate Hill. (If you've parked along the seafront, turn right with your back to the sea and head past the Compass Fountain, taking the next left-hand turn up Cargate Hill.) In 100m you'll see an entrance to a park on your left. Take the steps up through the park and at the top turn left. At Belle Vue Street turn right and

keep ahead at the next junction to join Belle Vue Crescent. Turn left onto Station Avenue and then left again onto Station Approach or into the car park to return to the start.

17 Muston Sands
2 miles (3.3 km)

Start: The Beach, Filey. **Sat Nav:** YO14 9LA.
Parking: Some free parking along the seafront, The Beach, or on Cargate Hill.
OS Map: Explorer 301 Scarborough, Bridlington & Flamborough Head. **Grid Ref:** TA119804.
Terrain: A mixture of muddy tracks and sandy beach. Not suitable for prams. The beach is great for dogs but there are some seasonal limitations.
Note – The beach is very wide but check tide times before you set off.
⊕ www.tidetimes.org.uk/filey-bay-tide-times

WALK HIGHLIGHTS
This is a wonderful coastal walk across a wide sandy beach, with the return leg along the cliff top, delivering sea breezes and great views throughout. Filey is worth exploring after the walk and there is plenty to see. Look out for the Compass Rose Fountain on the promenade which was part of a regeneration of the area which took place in the 2000s. The town was

20 Circular Walks in North & East Yorkshire

originally developed as a tourist destination in the 18th century as a quieter alternative to Scarborough but it was the development of the railway in 1846 that accelerated its growth.

REFRESHMENTS
Plenty in Filey. Walk up Cargate Hill and turn left through Crescent Gardens to reach Belle Vue Street, where there are a number of excellent options.

THE WALK
❶ Make your way to the Promenade and turn right, heading south. Keep ahead to reach The Paddling Pool where you join the beach and again turn right. Once past the end of the promenade this is Muston Sands. Keep walking along the beach for approx. ¾ mile and then look out for a slipway off to the right, known as Mile Haven. Turn right to leave the beach, and almost immediately look out for a footpath sign and steep steps off to the right. Go up the steps then follow the path as it bends right to continue to the top of the cliffs.

❷ At the top follow the path that runs alongside the golf course back towards Filey. As you get closer to Filey, cross a footbridge, then head down some steps. Cross a further bridge to join a tarmac track. Turn right towards the sea to reach the promenade and return to the start.

Walk 17 – **Muston Sands**

18 Flamborough Head
5½ miles (9 km)

Start: South Landing Car Park, South Sea Road, Flamborough.
  Sat Nav: YO15 1AG.
Parking: South Landing Car Park (pay & display). There is also some limited free parking along the approach road to the car park.
OS Map: Explorer 301 Scarborough, Bridlington & Flamborough Head.
  Grid Ref: TA230695.
Terrain: Paved road, gravel and muddy paths. The route is undulating along cliffs with some optional steep steps. No stiles. Suitable for dogs.

WALK HIGHLIGHTS

This route offers a thrilling cliff walk with great views, geology, art, history and wildlife. It starts along the Flamborough Young Roots Sculpture Trail where there is a series of sculptures inspired by local stories and legends. At the headland you'll see an impressive natural rock formation in the shape of a dinosaur as well as not one but two lighthouses. The original lighthouse was built in 1669 but was never lit. In 1806 the newer lighthouse was

Walk 18 – **Flamborough Head**

built and is still in use today. Flamborough Head also has one of the most important seabird colonies in Europe. In early summer the cliffs are packed with breeding birds including puffins, and seals can often be seen off the coast all year round.

REFRESHMENTS
There are cafés at Flamborough Head.

THE WALK
1 Exit to the rear of the car park, heading through a metal farm gate. The level path, known as the Sculpture Trail, leads into woods and then reaches a metal bridge. Cross the bridge and then follow the route off to the left. Note the artwork along the route. The path skirts the edge of the field and then reaches the coast.

2 At the Lighthouse Sculpture turn left, and follow the undulating path along the cliff edge for approx. 2 miles. This path is easy to follow and continues on as the old and new lighthouses become more visible. When closer to

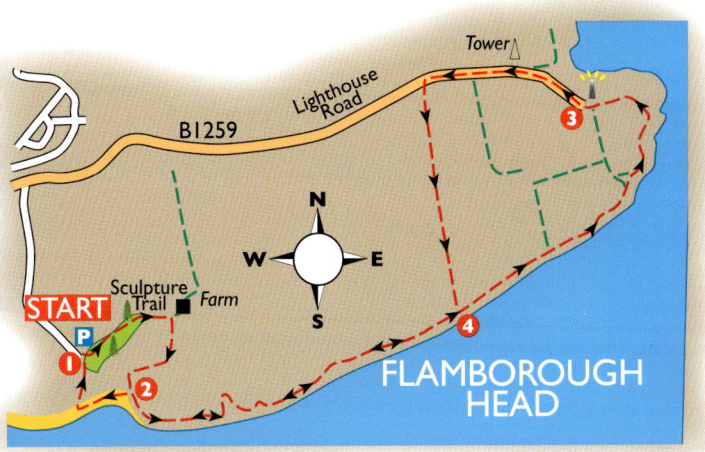

20 Circular Walks in North & East Yorkshire

Flamborough Head, a number of paths join the route. Simply continue along the most seaward path, this eventually arrives at the 'Head' and offers spectacular views. Look to your right and you'll see what is known as The Drinking Dinosaur, an amazing rock formation in the sea. Continue towards the radio masts then follow the tarmac road to pass the newer lighthouse.

❸ Once past the lighthouse turn right and follow the road round to the left to pass the shops/café. Keep ahead towards the old lighthouse, and then continue along the road for a further 200m to reach a footpath sign off to the left. Follow this through a gap in the hedge, the path initially runs parallel to the road but bends away to cross fields towards the cliffs. This can be muddy.

❹ The path reaches a T-junction with other paths, simply turn right to retrace your steps back along the coast towards the car park. When the path reaches the Lighthouse Sculpture again do not retrace your steps but continue along the path ahead keeping the sea to your left. This path bends right into woods and then reaches a branch off to the left to some steep steps. Turn left to descend the steps to arrive at the RNLI station and the beach. Once tired of the beach ascend the road to arrive at the start point.

19 Sewerby to Danes Dyke

2½ miles (4 km)

Start: Sewerby (Picnic) Car Park, Sewerby Road. **Sat Nav:** YO15 1EL.
Parking: Sewerby (Picnic) Car Park (pay & display).
OS Map: Explorer 301 Scarborough, Bridlington & Flamborough Head. **Grid Ref:** TA199686.
Terrain: Grassy paths and muddy tracks. The route is gentle but not suitable for prams. No stiles. Dog-friendly.

WALK HIGHLIGHTS

This gentle walk along the East Riding Heritage Way takes in wide open parkland and plenty of coastal views. You then skirt the edge of Danes Dyke Local Nature Reserve, once a smugglers' inlet, which got its name from the ancient ditch and bank earthwork which runs through the reserve. There is mystery as to why it was dug here but the structure resembles defensive works found elsewhere in England (Aberford Dykes in West Yorkshire) so that seems the most likely reason. There is also debate over when it was constructed, some historians believe it to be Iron Age but the general thinking is it is likely to be post Roman. The ditch is visible in the woods between points 2 and 3 on the walk.

20 Circular Walks in North & East Yorkshire

REFRESHMENTS
The Old Forge, just a short walk from the car park (turn right along Main Street), has outside seating, a good menu with plenty of pub classics and sea views. Dog-friendly.
☎ 01262 601111 ⊕ www.theoldforgesewerby.co.uk

THE WALK
❶ From the back of the car park head towards the sea. At the coast path turn left, with the sea to your right and follow the tarmac track until it

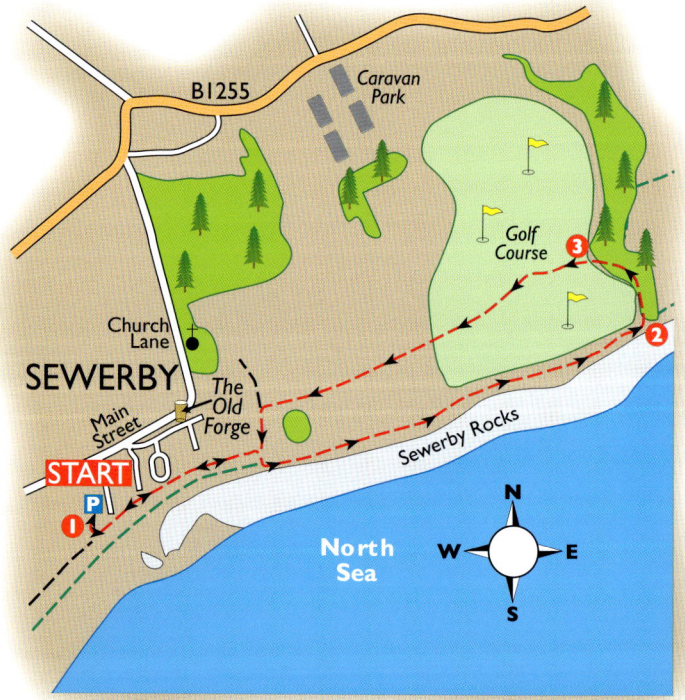

Walk 19 – **Sewerby to Danes Dyke**

curves to the left in approx. 500m. At this point keep right to walk behind the cricket pitch benches to join the muddier path nearer the cliff edge. Here the path is fenced from the cliffs. Look to your left and you'll see Georgian Grade I listed Sewerby Hall on the other side of the cricket pitch. This path continues north and follows a route between the cliffs and a golf course.

❷ The path reaches the end of the golf course at the edge of some woods, part of Danes Dyke Local Nature Reserve, and trends left to go inland, along the edge of the woods. Follow this path as it enters the woods and joins another path, where you turn left (signposted car park/nature trail). Keep to the path as it gently ascends to another junction.

❸ Turn left to follow the bridleway in the direction of Sewerby. The bridleway exits the woods and passes between gorse bushes across the edge of the golf course. It passes a Second World War pillbox, the design of which is unique to the north-east of England, and eventually leaves the golf course to reach an open grassy area. Keep ahead to skirt the cricket pitch and then turn left back towards the coast path. At the cliffs turn right to return to the start.

20 Barmston

3 miles (5.5 km)

Start: Sands Lane, Barmston. **Sat Nav:** YO25 8PG.
Parking: Roadside near the Black Bull Retreat on Sands Lane.
OS Map: Explorer 295 Bridlington, Driffield & Hornsea.
  Grid Ref: TA163591.
Terrain: A mixture of very muddy tracks and some paved roads. Not suitable for prams but good for dogs. Not recommended if very wet as the fields are low lying.

WALK HIGHLIGHTS

A peaceful walk of two halves, the first is a quiet walk across low lying farmland while the second is closer to the coast and offers wonderful views towards the Flamborough peninsula.

Erosion is a real problem along this part of the Yorkshire coast so this walk does not follow any cliff edges or beach. The soft clay means that the cliffs erode at between 4ft to 8ft per year. It is estimated that the coast was

Walk 20 – **Barmston**

a further 3½ miles out to sea during Roman times and it is thought that as many as thirty villages have been lost along this short coastline (between Bridlington and Spurn point).

REFRESHMENTS
The Black Bull Retreat is part of a luxury lodge complex but also welcomes local walkers.

THE WALK

1 To the right of the Black Bull Retreat on Sands Lane you'll find a footpath sign leading towards Barmston Methodist Church. Follow the path past the church then through a gate into a field. Head across the field towards a stand of trees and continue out the other side, over another field to reach a rickety wooden footbridge which you cross. This is the Barmston Main Drain, which is actually quite wide so calling it a drain does not do it justice. At the far side of the bridge turn left then immediately right to continue along the path as it follows a line of trees and hedge that act as the field boundary. The path starts to curve gently to the left at the end of the hedge, then meets a crossing of tracks. Follow the track straight ahead, keeping a large hedge to your right.

2 In 400m the track approaches some houses and passes a 30mph sign. Follow the track as it bends sharply left and then in 20m, it turns sharply right. Here, look for a yellow sign off to the left, marking a public right of way. Head for the yellow sign and pick up the path as it goes through a hedge then turns right to follow the edge of the field. Follow the path keeping the houses and then holiday homes to the right. After approx. 250m turn left by a footpath sign to cross a field. This then reaches a hedge and joins a track at a T junction. Turn right to the end of the track, only 10m further, then follow the slight left turn to now follow a faint footpath along a boundary between fields (note the lone tree ahead). Follow this path until it meets the drain. At the drain, turn right and then turn left to use the wide bridge to cross over it. Along this part of the walk enjoy the views towards Bridlington and Flamborough Head.

3 Once over the drain, follow the signed clear track visible ahead crossing a field towards the village. The track leads between houses and through a gate, onto Southfields Lane. At the end of the lane turn left to return to your car.

20 Circular Walks in North & East Yorkshire